The Freedom Blueprint

Jude Mendonsa

Copyright © 2019
Jude Mendonsa
The Freedom Blueprint
All rights reserved.

No part of this publication may be reproduced, distributed, or transmitted in any form or by any means, including photocopying, recording, or other electronic or mechanical methods, without the prior written permission of the publisher, except in the case of brief quotations embodied in critical reviews and certain other non-commercial uses permitted by copyright law.

Jude Mendonsa

Printed in the United States of America
First Printing 2019
First Edition 2019

10 9 8 7 6 5 4 3 2 1

"Compound interest is the eighth wonder of the world. He who understands it, earns it…He who doesn't…pays it."

Albert Einstein

Table of Contents

- Introduction 1
- Chapter 1 3
  - Wealth: What Is It? 3
- Chapter 2 9
  - Wealthy Thinking 9
  - Money vs Time 11
  - The Mindset of the Wealthy 13
- Chapter 3 19
  - Financial Responsibility 19
  - How Does the Money Go? 20
  - Cash 21
  - Loans 22
  - Credit Cards 24
  - Wants vs Needs 26
  - Control Spending, Live Below Your Means 28
- Chapter 4 33
  - Invest? Start with Yourself 33
  - Increase Your Knowledge 35
  - Change Your Circle 37
  - Take Care of Your Time 39
  - Physical Health 40
  - A Hustle 41
- Chapter 5 43

- Types of Freedom 43
  - A. Cashflow – Freedom from Money 45
  - B. Understanding Good Debt – The Freedom from Bad Debt 47
  - C. Know Your Worth – Freedom of Time 49
- Chapter 6 53
  - Make Your Money Work! 53
  - The Market 55
  - Real Estate Investing 59
  - Business Investing 63
  - Ecommerce 64
  - Traditional Business 66
  - 1. An Idea 67
  - 2. Create a Plan 68
  - 3. Financing 69
  - 4. Get the Word Out 71
  - 5. Business setup 73
  - 6. Develop a Team 74
- Chapter 7 77
  - Focus Your Effort 77
- Chapter 8 81
  - Protect Your Wealth 81
- Chapter 9 89
  - Plan Your Dreams and Seize Them 89

INTRODUCTION

This book was written for the budding entrepreneur who does not know where to start. The Business owner who knows there is more than just working seven days a week from morning till night.

When I first started in business I had no idea of how to become successful. What steps to take to get started, who to ask for help, or how to even open a bank account. Looking back now that I understand the power of mentors I wished I would have had someone to lean on and guide me. I wrote this book hoping to help many of you that were just like me.

This is meant to be a guide to help get you started on a path to building wealth. No matter if you want to start a business, flip real estate, or learn to invest for a better future this book will have something for you.

CHAPTER 1
WEALTH: WHAT IS IT?

Wealth can mean many different things to people. If you ask some people, "what is it to be wealthy?" They will give examples like to have millions of dollars, exotic cars, or more than one house. Some will say it is time, or freedom of choice. Others will say it's all of it, the ability to do whatever you want whenever you want without the constraints of money or time. When I was young, I always thought of being wealthy, or being rich, as having millions of dollars, a big house, and fast cars. I wanted that rap star lifestyle. To be able to go on huge spending sprees, buy the newest cars and the top hotel rooms, and eat and drink the finest of foods and liquors.

What I didn't realize at the time though, was that *rich* is just another version of poor. I know your already thinking "what? Is he crazy?" Well, let me explain. You see, there is a big difference between *rich* and *wealthy*. Yes, both may have the ability to buy whatever home, car, or trip they want. But the difference comes down to how their money is obtained and controlled thereafter.

You see the rich, much like the poor, work for their money. The rich also have many liabilities like the poor – very expensive liabilities. The rich rely on their job just like the poor, and when that job disappears, so do the cars, houses, trips etc.

How many times have we seen a professional athlete or movie star who has made millions reach a slow-down in their career – or even worse, lose their career – and then have to file bankruptcy or became penniless. Look at Mike Tyson, who made $400 million in his career. After some challenges in life and bumps in the ring, he had lost it all and filed bankruptcy. Or Nicolas Cage, known as one of Hollywood's charitable stars. He had homes and castles all over the world, as well as a collection of some of the most sought-after comic books. He was listed as one of the highest paid actors on Forbes, only to have to sell off most of his homes and collections. You can see he took every action he could to help pay back debts and tax bills.

These stories happen time and time again. People will win the lottery, only to be in a worse position a few years later. Friends will get a really good paying job, only to over leverage themselves with the new truck, boat, or house. And it's not necessarily their faults. We aren't taught what true wealth is, how to invest, how to control our money. Instead we are continuously attacked with sales ads to keep up with the neighbors and music videos pushing the lavish lifestyle of the famous.

Well the wealthy, unlike the rich, don't rely on an earned income. The wealthy instead learn how to invest and leverage their money to work for them through different streams of income. When a rich person loses their income, it's over. But When a wealthy person loses a stream of income, they usually have three to six more still working for them.

The wealthy have learned that time is their most valuable asset, so they work and invest to protect it and give themselves the biggest return of more time they can. The rich and poor instead look at money as the most important and trade time foolishly for it and the pursuit of liabilities.

I had a gentleman in my life that I thought of as a mentor for a while. I wanted to learn from him because he was RICH. He had all the things: the Escalades, the old sports cars, boats, motorcycles, a massive 10,000+

square foot house, etc. He had multiple businesses and invested in flipping real estate and buying and flipping cars.

What I failed to see though, was that even though he may of been rich, he wasn't wealthy. He worked 90+ hours a week. His kids spent most their time sitting in an Escalade watching TV while their parents worked. Everything he did, even though he had many streams of income, all relied on him putting in hours.He ended up going through a depression and getting sick. When that happened, they lost everything in a relatively short amount of time. Once the trading of time for dollars stopped, so did the cashflow.

The wealthy have knowledge the rich do not. The wealthy understand...

- **How money works and how to make it grow.**
- **How to trade money for money.**
- **How to leverage other people's efforts for money.**
- **How to create multiple streams of income that flow.**
- **How generational wealth and building a dynasty work.**
- **How to create systems to grow their wealth and network of assets.**

When the wealthy decide to stop, or if there is an uncontrollable reason the cashflow doesn't happen, the wealthy have trained their money to keep doing the work. I like the line Kevin O'Leary always uses on Shark Tank, where he describes his money as little soldiers. And when he sends his soldiers off to war, he expects them to come back with prisoners.

The gentleman I spoke of didn't have the financial literacy that the wealthy have. He understood hard work and how to find money in different avenues. But he didn't know how to create streams of cash that would consistently flow back into his pocket.

The rich, like my friend, are like the poor in a lot of ways. They live for the weekend and how many things they can acquire. Yes, their weekends are more extravagant, and their toys are cooler. But still, they are motivated by money and the fun to be had from it.

The wealthy are motivated by their purpose, passion, and dreams. The wealthy are living and building for the future generations. I've always been told by my mentors that it is important to plan *generationally*. We should always plan at least 3 generations ahead. Look at the Rothschilds, a family dynasty that came up from squalor to become one of the wealthiest families ever. Mayer Amschel Rothschild was born on the 23rd of February 1774, in a Jewish ghetto – one of eight children.

He grew up to become a moneychanger/banker. Mayer understood generational wealth, so he raised his children to continue on in the family business, expanding an international banking system throughout Europe. You can see that through a knowledge of compound interest and generational wealth education, the Rothschild family has continued to flourish 270+ years later.

Again, the rich may plan further ahead than the poor and have better retirement plans, but the rich and poor still rely on incomes from jobs. The wealthy plan things out to have a generational residual income so that even their children's children may have freedom of time. Being *rich* is having lots of money to be able to afford lots of liabilities, while being *wealthy* is having residual streams of income that allow you the time to enjoy and have whatever you want in life. Being wealthy is having not an abundance of time, but the ability to enjoy your precious time to its fullest extent.I, like so many others, wanted to be rich. I never understood what true wealth was. The understanding of the value of time vs money never entered my realm of thought. Because of that, I made many mistakes in my youth that kept me poor no matter how much money I made.

My dad was always about the quick money. He and my uncle had a drug operation where they made around a million dollars in profit in under one year. But my dad liked toys and trips. We got to have a lot of fun when I was young. But one day when I was around 7, it all came to a stop. My dad got raided. After that there was nothing left. The cashflow stopped and so did our way of life. My mom and I had to move in with my grandmother, and then finally move into a beat-up trailer where we were so poor the only way my mom could clothe me was from hand-me-downs from friends.

My dad was worried about being rich and having toys. He also wanted to acquire the easy way through quick ill-gotten deals. Just like my rich friend, my dad traded time for dollars. Because of that, the first hiccup in the system (going to prison) meant no more money.

Instead of learning from my dad's mistakes and idiocy, all I learned was I wanted to be rich and not have to suffer without all the things in life I craved. I didn't have much growing up things-wise. My family loved me, but my clothes were always to small or had holes and stains. My shoes always fell apart. The glasses I wore were free old-people frames my grandma would find. So, when I grew up, all I wanted was fast cars, big houses, and lots of women. So some of my friends and I would do these deals to try and make big quick money like my dad did. We'd make twenty to thirty grand in a weekend and have nothing to show for it after words except maybe some memories of some parties – maybe. Even once I cleaned my life up and started getting better paying jobs, I just found more things to spend it on. I didn't understand investing or wealth creation. There was no financial literacy. I went years working hard twelve-hour days, and at the end of it all, nothing to show for it.

If I would have been financially educated and been taught the value of time over just having things, I would've been able to make better choices to actually affect my future freedom and wealth. If only I would've understood the value of time vs money and that we only have so much to trade.

CHAPTER 2
WEALTHY THINKING

Step one on your journey to wealth will be this: "**CHANGE YOUR STINKING THINKING.**"

Our minds have been programmed for so long in all the wrong ways. You have been told for so long to do good at school so you can get into a good college, so you can get a good job. And then you get to work for forty more years at that job so you can hopefully have ten to twenty years of retirement. Also, that retirement comes with a monthly stipend of about a third or less than what you were trying to live off of when you were working. That's even if there is still social security when you get to that age.

What a lie the American dream has become. The best way I can think to explain it is to look at the movie *The Matrix*. Imagine you are Neo, a drone who has been given little information except what it takes to be a drone in today's society, working your life away. And yet you have this feeling – a feeling that there is more to life, that this isn't everything you were designed for. You know you want more, so you start searching. Well, because of your searching, you came across me – your Morpheus.

Now it is my duty to help you see the light and that there is a better way. A way where you can have unlimited wealth, unlimited time, and the ability to enjoy it sooner than later. It will be your duty to decide, like Neo, to grab hold of this new reality and change your life, or to accept your old life and stay the course you're on, and maybe enjoy the last feeble years of your life.

You must start to see and think as the wealthy do. If we continue to think that a job (just over broke) will provide us the life we desire, we will always be let down. And the problem is as you get older, it will get harder to correct your course. Not saying it can't be done at any age, but hey, why wait?

MONEY VS TIME

The first thing to change in our poor thinking is our understanding of what's truly valuable. For most of us – whether middle class, poor or even rich – we look at money as the most valuable thing there is because it is how we pay for our wants and needs. We tell ourselves, "If I have more money, I can get more wants and have fewer needs."

We aren't taught the true value of time vs money. Time is our truest and most valuable asset. We don't use money to get wants and needs, we actually use time. We are all traders; not in stocks, bonds, or baseball cards, but traders of *time*. The rich and poor are constantly in a battle of trading time for money to trade for things. The wealthy are in a position where they are leveraging money and others' efforts so they can have more time.

God gave us time as a special gift, and we have only been given a certain amount of it so that we would cherish it – not waste it slaving for dollars to get trinkets. Our time is meant to be spent with loved ones and enjoying this wonderful world that was created for us – to go out and glorify Him and one another.

Most of us just understand that we are here to work and pay taxes, and once we reach a certain age, we get a little stipend to lay around till we die. I actually have friends who still believe this! This poor mindset is a cancer on society that must be eradicated through education. <u>The poor waste so much time. They are focused on entertainment, dreaming of the next thing, and even making money. How many hours a day do you watch TV? Play video games? Daydream?</u> There are even so-called successful people that waste time. You will see them always so busy just going non-stop. If you look closely, you'll see that they are busy being busy and not actually being productive – busy wasting time. So, at this point, I'd like you to take a few minutes to close your eyes and look deeply at what you do daily. Is it being profitable with your time and leading to more time in the future? Or are you just throwing it away until one day you realize there is no time left?

Now take a few more minutes and think about all the things you could do and enjoy without it being a waste of your most valuable resource if you were wealthy. If you had residual wealth and could take time to yourself what would you do? Where would you be? Who would you spend time with? If you are like the majority of people, you are probably in a position where you are working way too much and then spending your off time in front of a tv - only to have to wake up and do it all over again the next day. Hoping that one day you'll make it to retirement and not be completely disgruntled about where you are in life.

Now how much better would it be to create wealth and have the time to do anything and everything you desire to accomplish with your life? To be free with your time? To be able to bless the loved ones around you with your time?

We only have so much time in our account. Each and every day our time account depletes a little more. There is no way to extend it, so we must make choices that will lead to being able to use as much of it as possible and to the fullest extent we can. You can't trade your time for wealth and financial freedom - I hope you are starting to see that the only path to wealth is separating your time from money, and that what you really desire is freedom of time and not just money and more "liabilities".

The Mindset of the Wealthy

To begin the journey on the road to wealth, the first thing to work on is our poor mindset. You are now hopefully beginning to understand that trading time for dollars is a misguided perspective that has no benefit to you. So, the first challenge becomes changing our mindset to a wealthy one – a mindset of abundant thinking.

As you read these next items, I encourage you to really listen to your inner voice as you explore these new concepts. Take in the full value and importance here, and become consciously aware of how these ideas resonate with you and your current reality.

1: Understand your worth. I used to trade my time for six dollars an hour. That means I would sell you one hour of my life for a paltry six bucks. That is less than a value meal at a fast food restaurant. At this point in my life, I won't do anything for less than hundreds or thousands of dollars an hour. In truth, my worth is infinitely valuable – especially the older I get because there is less time left, and as I get more financially educated, I earn more by refusing to trade time and instead focus on cashflow. So, ask yourself, how much is your time worth? That hour you gave away for ten, twenty, even a hundred dollars, was it really worth it?

2. Money is a tool. Yes, you may have to trade some time at the beginning to obtain money, but once you do, it's time to put the tool to work for you! The wealthy understand that and apply it liberally. You could almost look at the wealthy as orchard farmers. They take their money and plant it in different assets and investments growing "money trees." With a little care, the money grows into big, tall investments that offer the wealthy a generous harvest.

3. Long term thinking. A wealthy mindset is one of long-term thinking. The poor only think to the weekend. The rich maybe think to retirement. The wealthy think generationally. As we saw in the example of the Rothschild dynasty, we must be thinking about the future generations. It can be looked at like a good chess strategy. You plan out twenty moves ahead and plan different variations for different outcomes. You must plan today, RIGHT NOW, for your tomorrow. If you don't start thinking on it now, it will never happen.

4. Patient gratification. A wealthy person doesn't go after the instant gratification. Building wealth takes time and hard work. We have to break the mindset so many of the poor and rich have – the mindset of, "I want it now!" so they either go finance it or spend what they should've invested, or even worse, they just give up on ever having it because they can't wait. Its ok to suffer today for the benefit of tomorrow. We don't worry about temporary comforts now so we can have long term satisfaction later.

5. Build a team – don't do it all on your own. It's a poor mindset to think you have to do it all yourself. The "rich" man I mentioned before refused to let anyone else do anything. That was one of his biggest follies. I came from working in corporate restaurants and I would always ask, "why won't you let your managers do anything?" He was always worried about being taken advantage of, and because of this he could only grow so far – he was his own "bottleneck." The wealthy build teams *and* trust those teams. They leverage their team to maximize everything. Ray Croc didn't worry about training managers and them stealing the idea and starting a competing restaurants. He just focused on building teams and inspiring them to build the dream. Don't do it all on your own. Build a team!

6. "How can I afford it?" The poor always think, "I can't afford that." The rich just finance it. But the wealthy ask, "how can I afford that?" A person with an abundant mindset will look at, let's say, a new sports car, and figure out a way to get a new asset to cover that expense. The wealthy don't let anything hold them back. The wealthy solve problems and get the house, car, trip, and ultimately the freedom they want.

7. Gratitude. I learned this one from Tony Robbins – and he heard it from billionaire investor Sir John Templeton. Having an attitude of gratitude is true wealth. If you have a billion dollars, but you're angry, you will have a horrible life even though you can have anything you want. This point is well illustrated by the island countries like Fiji, where people don't have a lot of money, or anything for that matter, but they are genuinely grateful for the beautiful world they are in.

8. Wanting More. We have been trained and conditioned to believe that wanting more is morally wrong and selfish. That having too much money is bad. The wealthy, on the other hand, look at it this way – is it wrong to want more time with your kids? Is it wrong to want to get closer to your spouse? Is it wrong to want more time to devote to God or helping the less fortunate? No, it is not wrong to want any of these things. The wealthy have a mindset that more time means more being able to enjoy the important things in life and being able to devote more of themselves to family or others. It's ok to want more.

Take a moment and consider what the true consequences will be if you keep going the direction you are. Even if you max out retirement accounts, what would happen to your life if you fell sick or were injured for 6 months? Would you have to use up all your savings – if you have any? Many would be losing their car, or even their home, and relying on friends and family to help them stay afloat. No one but you is interested in giving you the time and future you desire.

Do you want anyone else to have control over your financial destiny? Even the idea of a social security retirement is gone. And why would you want to wait until you are too old and brittle to go enjoy life to retire anyways? You must change your mindset and understanding of money. I cannot stress enough how critical it is to understand that the way of life we've been taught will never lead to freedom. We are taught to be drones and slaves to the system – to sell our time to the people that understand how valuable it actually is for pennies. With proper financial literacy, you can break out from the money matrix we are in and start to work around the system the same way the wealthy do.

People today are not mentally trained to become wealthy. It is important that you make mindset your first major change in life on your way to financial freedom. Many people are trained to have negative emotions towards money, thinking it is evil. Again, money is a tool, nothing more. What you do with it is either good or evil. The idea that money is evil is nothing more than a misguided observation of how little most people actually value themselves. But enough talk, let's do some exercises here to start the mental change. If you are serious about taking action RIGHT NOW to make real change in yourself, follow along and do the following exercises.

Step 1: Close your eyes and think about the pain in your life right now that stems from not having enough money and trying to solve this by trading your time for it. Do you lose out on hanging with friends and family? Are you always stuck telling your kids or loved one "maybe someday?" Are you scared that you can't take that drive because your car may break down? Find the most painful things in your life that you cannot change because of a lack of money.

Step 2: I want you to now make the connection of pleasure to money. Imagine that you now have the right amount of wealth. Create a detailed mental image of what that looks like for you – living your life the way you desire to. Pay close attention in this metal picture to how much time and freedom you have. How many people and charities are you able to help? What trips are you going on? What hobbies are you now able to partake in?

You'll find in this book that I often repeat the phrase, "we will always try to avoid pain and look to pleasure." Why do so many people lounge about instead of working hard? Because it's more pleasurable right now in this moment. So you have to make the mental connection in your mindset that being broke and not having freedom is not pleasurable, but reaching your goals is true pleasure in life.

Step 3: You need to see how wealthy you already are. The more positive and passionate we are, the more it attracts those same things around us. Nobody wants to work with a downer that's always moving from a place of, "Man, being broke sucks, I can't wait to be rich." People are drawn to working with the person that goes "Man I love life and all my blessings, and I am so excited that as my wealth grows, I get to help more people." Every day you must make the mental connection that you are wealthy and push that out into the world around you. It is your job to make this your life.

"But Jude," you might be asking, "how can I say I'm already wealthy when I have nothing and everything sucks?"

Just the fact you are alive is a blessing. Every breath you get is one that someone on their last would give anything to take. But even more, if you live in a first world country, especially if you are in America or Canada, look around you. You have roads. You have libraries. You get to believe what you want and say what you want. You don't have to walk miles for water. If you are reading this book and you are wealthy based on the simple fact you can read and are able to increase your knowledge whenever you want. You are amongst the most fortunate human beings in history to have the power to shape your own destiny to be whatever it is you chose to make it. How amazing and wealthy you already are!

Now make these mental connections and change your mindset to one of wealth. When you make this mental change, it will create synergy and everything else will start to change: Your interactions with people. How you deal with good and bad situations that come up. Your boss will notice a difference which will affect your work positively. Business partners and employees will notice and be motivated. Even your partner and kids will take notice and follow the change.

CHAPTER 3
FINANCIAL RESPONSIBILITY

The second steps you will take on the road to wealth will be learning how to be financially independent, and in the next chapter we will expand on these concepts to show you the road to financial freedom. I differentiate the two, so you can have a more clear understanding of two schools of thought. Financial independence is the starting point from which all future wealth will grow. Put very simply, this is where you will learn and develop the skills to become debt-free and spend less than you make.

The first stage of financial independence is to begin exercising control over outgoing cashflow. The second stage of financial freedom begins when your residual wealth/cashflow exceeds your spending and covers the life you want to live. Financial freedom controls both incoming and outgoing cashflow. You will soon understand that it's not what you own, it's what you control that's important.

Normally I don't talk much about financial independence. Being a stepping stone to wealth, this subject is often overlooked by most of the "experts" out there simply because the wealthy operate under the assumption that this area is already in working order. We are going to discuss this here because this is a comprehensive guide book to wealth, and many of you are probably starting out with things like bad debt and poor spending habits. It will be easier if we find some ways to control bad spending and even find some hidden cash you didn't know you had monthly so we can use it to invest and create wealth.

How Does the Money Go?

First, we must understand how we spend and the different ways money leaves our pockets each month and keeps us from investing and saving. There are as many different ways we spend as there are people, but we can cover almost all of them by grouping them into 3 simple categories.

Cash

For many of us this is the toughest one to control. I always remember when I was young and getting money – whether it be from some chore I did, or hustling one of my friends into buying an old toy. I loved feeling that crisp new-to-me dollar. But what I loved even more was going to the local K-Mart down the road (sorry, I'm showing my age here) and buying something new with it right away.

Just like this youthful version of myself, many of us are not taught to save or invest. Instead we are taught, "If you want it, get it. You earned it so burn it. Treat yo'self." So as soon as we have cash, we spend it. Immediately going out to dinner, the movies, or drinking with friends. Buying the new phone, clothes, or games.

We see friends or ourselves get tax returns and immediately we are rich for all of about two seconds – then it's all gone till next year. It is so easy to part with cash. There is a nice thing about cash, though: when you run out, your spending is done. You can't burden yourself beyond running out of cash, unlike other spending methods that create long-term debt.

Loans

Loans are not as easily accessible as money, but it is still easy to get in over our heads with the wrong type of loan. We call this "bad debt." I will not be going into the argument of good debt vs bad debt here, so we will focus here on discussing bad debt. I've had many a friend growing up who found a new car they wanted and that they could simply get approved for a loan and have it immediately. All of the sudden, at eighteen years old, they were strapped with a $30,000 loan paying $500 or more a month while only making a little over minimum wage.

For many, they think of their parents having the nice house, the big truck, maybe a boat, but not realizing that it took years for them to get to that point. Us youth, with new-found buying power, use the power of loans unwisely to shortcut the path to earning the things we want.

We also are never aware of how much the banks leverage compound interest against us. A simple home loan of $150,000 over the life of the loan at a 3.5% interest turns into a total of $242,482. That's a loss of $92,000 – but most young adults are lead to believe that this is one of the best investments that we can make. It's easy to think we can afford something because the bank approves us, but rarely are we properly prepared for how these extra expenses truly impact our lives – especially if we get sick or lose a job.

Just because the bank says "approved" doesn't mean our budget should. Even worse than the car and home loans, we have real sharks out there giving out things like payday loans and pawn loans. The poor and financially uneducated fall into the traps of these things quite frequently due to over spending and trying to cover periods that we lack cash.

I mention these because they are some of the harshest of loans and bad debt, and you must stay vigilant to avoid these at all costs.

Credit Cards

Credit cards can be an amazing tool. For the smart investor, they can lead to free trips, instant money to close a deal, or even that emergency fund to fix something like a car problem or broken-down furnace. To the uneducated and the undisciplined, they can be a gateway to financial ruin. It's too easy to go somewhere and see something you want that you may not have the money for and think, "…hmm, I'll just use the card now and I can pay it off in no time." Before you know it, your card is maxed out and you have more payments than you know what to do with.

This is only made worse by the fact that when starting out, there is nothing easier than getting approved for credit cards. You basically have children who just became an adult yesterday that are now being trusted with the financial responsibility of money they don't even have – when they were never taught how to be responsible with the small amount of earning and spending power they do have. It is pretty easy to see how this is a such a direct route to financial ruin for so many.

When I was eighteen, I decided I wanted a video camera for a business idea I had. So, I hopped online and applied for a bunch of cards. Before I knew it, I had access to around $6,000 in purchasing power that I truly did not have. Keep in mind, I was bouncing between my Grandma's house and my car for living arrangements at this time. I should not have had these cards. Well within a short time, I had three maxed out cards. I had an awesome video camera, a new computer, and a surround sound system to connect to a friend's tv. What was I thinking? I only made $6.30 an hour at this point in time. I had a car loan, Insurance, and now these card payments. I went from a very positive, I-can-rule-the-world type of man, to an angry, stressed-out, bitter person in no time. Credit cards again can be an awesome tool. I use them in my businesses continuously. They provide free airfare, discounts on trips, and even help in an emergency.

But when I was young, they almost ruined me. Unlike a loan where you have to meet certain qualifications to get approved, there is almost a card out there for anyone in just about any situation. And card interest rates are un-Godly. It's one thing to pay a loan at 3-6% interest, but it's another thing entirely to pay at 15-29% interest. If you make your minimum car payment each month, you'll pay it off in three to five years depending on loan. But if you make minimum card payments, it can take five, ten, or fifteen years depending on the rate. That trinket you wanted now cost you the price of a car, or the down payment of your home.

Wants vs Needs

Most of what hurts our financial independence with debt is our weakness toward wants. When I got into that credit card debt I wasn't focused on my needs of food, education, or moving forward in life. I was focused on my wants and what could bring gratification right now. We are trained by marketing that we need all these things to fit in, be loved, have fun, etc. And so we automatically try to "keep up with the Joneses."Things as simple as wanting to fulfill the need of wanting something fast and tasty over wanting to prepare a healthy meal at home. If we eat at home, it can save money and keep us healthier and in better shape.

But that takes effort and planning, whereas it's so easy to go grab something quick and fried. The cost is higher to both your wallet and your health, but as you can see from living in a culture that has a fast food joint on every corner, we don't care about that. The want to feed a need now and get instant pleasure – that is more important.I have friends who do mission and humanitarian work all over the world. A good friend of mine, Mequel, pointed out a truth about this to me years ago. He was in the Philippines and what he noticed was people wouldn't have beds, they wouldn't have food, but they all had a cellphone. It didn't matter to them that they didn't have the need of a comfortable bed or proper nutrition. It mattered more to have the want satisfied of feeling like they had status because they owned a cell phone.

You can even see in a lot of Eastern European countries that are poor. The people will spend money on alcohol for the want of instant gratification to feel like they aren't suffering instead of investing in the need of education or business to change their life and actually take the difficult journey to get themselves out of the suffering. We will always focus more on pleasure over pain. So, we will choose quick pleasure even though it hurts us in the long run over suffering now, so we can have pleasure later.

So now take a few minutes and do a short exercise to reinforce this shift in your mindset. I want you to close your eyes and envision your life and where you'll be if you focus on wants now. What kind of pain will you be in later if you live wild and free now? If you don't start focusing on needs to better your life, how hard will life be? How sad will it be to be working non-stop to pay off debt at fifty-five years of age, or getting a door-greeter job in retirement to pay for your pain medication.

Write these down, and look back at them when you feel like selling your future short for a short-term pleasure now with negative consequences down the road. Now, take a couple minutes again and let's imagine the joy and freedom you'll have if you start focusing on what needs to be done now so you can have a life filled with wants later. How great will it be to enjoy an early retirement and travel the world because you were willing to sacrifice today so you could enjoy tomorrow?

We have to change our perspective on what causes pain and pleasure when it comes to financial responsibility. We will always want to do what is pleasurable over what is painful. So for many, fulfilling the wants of right now is pleasurable because tomorrow is so far away and the pain of tomorrow doesn't hurt as much as the pain of this moment. But if you really focus and see that making the decisions now that others won't will lead to much greater amounts of true pleasure in the future.

Control Spending, Live Below Your Means

So now that we have learned what methods we use to spend money and have an understanding of wants vs needs, we are going to do another exercise. The purpose of this will be to see where your money is going. We will find immediate things to cut out so we can start developing a savings at the end of each month – to begin taking the first steps on the path to creating true wealth.

In order to be able to be financially independent or even financially free, we must be able to control our spending and have an understanding of our incoming and outgoing cashflow and bills. A business would never be able to grow without proper accounting and knowing when it can purchase inventory or afford to hire more.

So, like a business, to grow or make purchases you should have an account of what your finances look like.So, if you've ever read a Ramsey book, you'll already have an idea of what we're going to be doing. This doesn't mean you can skip this part! This is truly the first step toward building real wealth, so take the steps. You will need to grab:

1. The last six months of bank statements and card statements.
2. Three highlighters of different colors. For example, we will use blue, yellow, and red.
3. A notebook.
4. Some testicular fortitude to be able to make some tough decisions for your future.

5. Some honesty to be willing to admit to your situation and where it's truly at.So, grab each statement and we are going to go line by line highlighting items.

- **Blue:** this one will be for needs. These are absolutes like rent/mortgage, utilities, groceries, if there was a real emergency (car broke down, home issue, etc.).
- **Yellow:** this will be for the middle areas. These are things that weren't really bad, but you still could've lived without. This will include eating out, a night at movies, fun with friends, etc. these are things that we enjoy and can be good, but could also be budgeted and used as rewards.
- **Red:** this is for 100% wasteful wants. These are things that are only for fulfilling today's wants and nothing for your future. Like going to the bar, buying doodads or clothing when unnecessary, any frivolous purchase.

After all is said and done, do three different rows, one for each color: blue for necessity, yellow for choices, and red for just wasteful spending. Count and put down how many lines are highlighted in each row. Then, put what the total of each color is in each row. Do this for each month you did so you can see the trends of what you spend.

From this point you will want to make some goals and budget yourself. We will start with three months of budget planning. Anything can be done easily enough for three months. This is why many workout programs go for three months or ninety days. It is just enough time where you're not mentally feeling overwhelmed, but it's also enough time to turn these changes into habits and start seeing progress.

1. Pay yourself first. As we get further into investing, this will become more and more important. The government understands this concept and that is why they get money out of your paycheck before you do. So, we will start with this. Your goal should be between 20-30%. At the beginning I understand something like 30% can seem near impossible so if you have higher debt to income ratio its ok to start at 10-20%. Never below 10% though. Out of every dollar you take in you need to put 10% of it away for investing. So, set your goal now of how much of your monthly income you will save. Write it down now.

2. Track your yellows. Set a goal for each month for your yellows going down in number. So, if you were averaging twenty yellow lines a month make your first month goal fifteen, then ten, and then five.

3. Get rid of red. Red will consist of the most frivolous expenditures, like going out drinking, or buying a new DVD or song on iTunes. These will usually be all credit card purchases as well. You must work hard to ensure these are eliminated as quick as possible. Each one of these is instant money back in your pocket.

4. Really analyze your blues and yellows as you go forward. Make sure all the needs in blue are for sure needs. You'll start to notice that you like saving money and building a nest egg, so you may discover things you can cut out in the grocery bill or ways to lessen the phone bill.

5. Destroy debt. Getting rid of bad debt will be the big push of financial independence. Make a tracking sheet of each debt showing how much you owe on each thing. Start with the lowest bill and do everything to pay it off first. Now take that payment and apply it to the next lowest. This is called snowballing. You will see your debt start to go down like dominos. Now on your tracking sheet you can map all this out to see exactly when things get paid off and when that debt-free day happens.

6. Don't be greedy. Set an amount to start paying forward. This is possibly the most important thing. As you start making sacrifices to help others, you will start to receive back tenfold. It doesn't have to be a lot at first. Start small at 2%, 5%, or 10%. But the amount of joy and wealth you will feel from doing this will cause a change that will attract more success to you. One of my mentor's goal is to give away 50%. I currently between tithe and charities give away around 30%. I do not say this to brag but to help motivate you. If you want to be where the successful are, you should do as they do.

Now you may not receive back from the same area where you give. Do not let this discourage you. As an example, we have some family that we always help. Some of them are the ones who just can't reciprocate it and others are the type that…well…are useless, but you love them anyways. Even though we give to them and we give to people in, let's say Africa, we never receive back from those areas. But I have friends who will at the drop of a hat come and fix my electrical if it goes out, no questions asked, and friends that will pick me up anywhere anytime if my car breaks down. And even financially through giving I have made awesome business connections where now I am working with some gentleman on ways to help bring more clean water to areas that don't have it. And through this project we are now discussing doing some business investments together.

So, give. Give your time. Give your love. Give your money. Give your passion and effort. These will help on your journey to more than financial independence. It will help towards your wealth.

Now this is a very minor chapter on budgeting and paying off debt. There are some amazing tools for getting rid of debt and budgeting out there. I am only writing the very basics in this book to help the person who doesn't know where to start. You can reach out to us at JudeMendonsa.com for more in-depth training and coaching, or look into things like: The Power of finance with Todd Fleming. He is a great friend of mine who is passionate about helping people break free. There are also great reading sources on these subjects by writers like Dave Ramsey and Lynnette Khalfani-Cox.

CHAPTER 4
INVEST? START WITH YOURSELF

Now that you've gone through your monthly budget and we've freed up some money, what do you do with it? Start investing, and the most powerful investment you can make is in yourself. This will also be one of the ways you pay yourself first, as we discussed in the last chapter. Jim Rohn said, "Find a way to add more value than anybody else does, and you'll never have to worry about anything. Every day, work harder on yourself than anything else, because if you become more intelligent, more valuable, more skilled – you can add more value to other people."

Markets crash, businesses go under, even empires fall. The only thing you can control in life is your own knowledge and abilities. If you invest in yourself daily by improving your skills, abilities, health, and I.Q., you are creating an investment that can never be taxed or taken away. And with these investments, you will never be at the limitations of others around you. If you pay too much in taxes, that's not your CPA's fault. They just do what their education taught them. It's your fault for not learning the strategies of the wealthy and making sure you're working with someone who can implement said strategies. It's not the government's fault social security won't provide you with your dream retirement. It's your fault for not understanding wealth building strategies and using them to take control of your own financial future.

It is so important that your first investments start in yourself. When you are on an airplane, what is it they say to do when the mask comes out in an emergency? "Put the mask on your own face first." The reason for this is if you try to take care of someone else first and then you pass out, you're no good to anyone after that – now you are a liability. The king needs to eat first so he has the energy to run the kingdom. The king needs to understand what issues are arising before any of the townspeople so he can come up with a plan to save the nation. Invest in you first so you can lead your empire to where it needs to go, and then once you're there, you can help others.

So now let's go over some ways to invest in ourselves first to help propel this journey to success and wealth.

Increase Your Knowledge

Obviously you're reading this now, so hopefully you are already doing this consistently. But maybe you're like I was and hate books and are only doing this right now because you were bribed or something. But reading is the number one way to start your growth. All the information in the world is out there in written form, and in most cases, you can even find it for free.

Because of books, you are also provided the opportunity to work with and learn from the greatest minds ever. You can be coached by Tony Robbins, Dale Carnegie, Robert Kiyosaki, even Jesus Christ. All the greatest minds ever want to see you successful, and because of that, they have written down advice, plans, and lessons from their journeys to help you out.

To be successful, it's important to do what the successful do. If you want a different life, you have to change from what hasn't been working and start doing what the successful do. If you look at the top CEOs and investors, most of them read an average of fifty books a year. So if you want to be a multi-millionaire, or billionaire, you should do as they do.I've always had trouble finding the time to read a book when I was poor-minded.

Now that I'm wealthy-minded, I realize how easy it truly is. Time block just fifteen minutes a day, or you can listen to an audio version. Another thing I found that really helps – and this may be a little personal – but download the book and read it whenever you go to the bathroom. It's amazing how much you can get read in your ten minutes sitting there, and for some men, even longer.I also recommend listening to podcasts.

Some of the greatest business minds of today have podcasts. Every week they are creating content free of charge to help you better yourself and grow. Take advantage of being able to learn from these individuals.

CHANGE YOUR CIRCLE

This is a tough one for many, but it is so important. You've heard the phrase, "birds of a feather flock together." If you haven't, or don't know what it means, what it's saying is that people hang out with someone they are like or want to be like. When someone is an ex-alcoholic or ex-drunk, but they keep hanging out with the same old friends every night in the bar or at the crack house, how long do you think they stay clean? They won't. They will fail. We have to change our circle so we are pressured to do better, not worse.

I used to be heavily into violence, sex, drugs, and just anything unprofitable. I tried getting better over and over, but I always continued hanging out with the same type of people. And overtime, things would get worse and worse until the summer of 2004 when I almost died from some horrible situations I put myself in. That was finally the start of my wakeup call. I realized if I kept going this direction with these people, I would end up dead or in prison.

I thank God that I had a grandma and an uncle that always pushed for me as a youth to grow up around our church. Because of having those influences, I was able to compare mine and my friends lives to those who were actually trying in life. I had one church friend who at my same age owned his own business, had an awesome truck, was traveling the world, and buying investment properties.

I realized my circle wasn't going to help me get where I really wanted to be. I left all those old friends and started hanging out with people who were where I wanted to be in life. And as I have continued to grow, I continue to increase the quality of my circle. If you want a better life, you must be influenced by those that have what you want, otherwise you will always be dragged down. Most of my old friends are still to this day doing the same things – bouncing from couch to couch, or even worse. Some are in prison or dead. You've also heard the term, "your network is your net worth?"

Well I cannot express how true that statement really is. As I have grown and continued to surround myself with better and more successful people my, opportunities have kept exploding. Invest in yourself by taking care of your circle and making sure only the right people are influencing you.

Take Care of Your Time

We have already learned that time is our most precious asset, so we need to properly take care of it. Start to manage it wisely by not wasting it on fruitless endeavors. Weigh things out and consider: "Does this conversation, tv show, or night of drinking help me toward my goals?" If not, then do away with it.

How often do you find yourself scrolling through Facebook posts or getting lost on a YouTube tangent? A great exercise to curb these things is to write down everything you did throughout the day, and then review it each evening. After doing that for a few days, you will naturally start to correct your behavior when you time waste. This will not only help in your personal life, but also in your professional life. The majority of people working an eight-hour day are only productive two hours and fifty-three minutes of the day. What a waste of your life, of your precious gift.

After auditing your time, I recommend creating a schedule, or time blocking so you can get the most out of your time. We want to maximize our efforts so we can reach our goals and hopefully obtain freedom, so we have more time for enjoying our pleasures.

Physical Health

What is the point of having money and freedom of time if your body gives out and you cannot enjoy it? Our physical body is just as important as our time. If the body is not taken care of, it will greatly diminish our time, or the quality of the time we get. We should have a focus on exercising regularly and maintaining a healthy diet.

Doing these things will increase our energy and give a better night's rest, which leads to more productivity and better moods. It helps us fight disease and have lasting health. Make sure in your scheduling to put in time for physical exercise. It doesn't have to be much. Even just fifteen to thirty minutes a day will change your world.

There are great resources out there between books, YouTube videos, or even following a fitness coach like my good friend Chad Molyneux, or many others online to learn different workout and meal plans. Your body is a machine and just like your car, if you don't give it proper maintenance or fuel, it will break down. Unlike a car though, you cannot go out and get new parts. Once it's done it's done, so let us take care of it for as long as we can.

A Hustle

A great way to invest in oneself is to start something to generate more income. A side hustle or business. Beyond another source of income, it is also a great way to increase your skills and learn new things. Running a business, you will have to grow in many aspects such as time management, leadership, communications, tactics, and planning.

All of this will help you grow as a person reaching a higher potential.If you do well with this side hustle or business, it can replace your normal nine to five and hopefully send you down a better path to reach freedom and wealth. Nothing provides returns like running your own business with so many of the benefits being beyond just money.

CHAPTER 5
TYPES OF FREEDOM

I'm not going to lie. I am so excited to write this part right here. I am not very fond of financial independence. I am a fan of financial FREEDOM! I LOVE FREEDOM!!!! Freedom is what America was founded on. Freedom is one of the biggest concepts of Christianity.

Why wouldn't someone rather be free? Slavery sucks. And slaves are what most of you are. Waking up everyday to go to your job to sell blocks of your life away hour by hour. For what – a bi-weekly paycheck that gives you just enough to scratch by until the next check? Yuck! Who wants to live like that? I'd rather be financially free. Free to be able to dictate my time and how it is spent. Free to decide if I'm going to work today or not. Free to take my kids on a trip just because we felt like it that day. Free to take time and spend it with a loved one if they are sick or just distraught.

I know I'm starting to repeat myself, but **"repetition is the mother of learning, the father of action, which makes it the architect of accomplishment"** —Zig Ziglar. And you really need this concept to sink into your mindset. Financial independence – being debt-free – is great, but debt-free will never get you freedom, true wealth. Even with a large savings, each year inflation and monthly needs eat away at it till there is nothing left. And God forbid a calamity happens. You don't have a spending problem, you have a cashflow problem. You don't have an ability to afford problem, you have a cashflow problem. You need residual cashflow, and you need it to grow to the size of life you want.

In another chapter, I went over mine and my wife's spending issues when it came to things like eating out or fun. We chose to start budgeting and paying off bills. And that is fine and good to learn financial responsibility as well as get rid of bad debt. But to live a life of scarcity and frugality, never experiencing much of anything, is no life at all. So, we had a mental change. Instead, we decided to pick a lifestyle we wanted with trips, fine dining, time off, etc., and build the cashflow so we could have it.

The wealthy have a mindset of abundance. More life, more time, more experiences. The poor are set on trying to pay off debt, save up for this, maybe do that one day. I don't want a life of maybes or wish-I-would-haves or maybe-next-times. I want life abundance, and you should too.Many of you reading this I'm sure are screaming, "Yes, I want more but how do I get it? How do I build cashflow?" Well first, let's go over some concepts to help open your mind for cashflow. The concepts of freedom from money, freedom from debt, and freedom from time.

A. Cashflow – Freedom from Money

Taylor Peugh is a good friend, mentor, and leader who I look up to. And he is so brilliant about this concept. He is focused on one massive thing at every moment, and that is increasing his cashflow. I have seen him when someone brings something negative his way like drama or gossip. He'll just look at them and say "Will this help me increase my cashflow? No? Then I don't want to hear it."

We must be this way about our dreams and goals. Laser-focused to where we let nothing get in the way or interrupt the journey. So many people never achieve anything because they lose focus. They fall into the mundane. You have to become laser-focused about what you want if you ever hope to get out of the life you are in and into the life you want. The easiest way to do that is to first make cashflow your focus. Once you have enough cashflow, you can do anything. You will have freedom of time, which leads to a lot of opportunity. For me, it was easiest to figure out my goal life, which at the time was $30,000 a month in residual cashflow. With that I could have $10,000 to devote to God and charities, $10,000 to devote to continual investing (growing cashflow), and $10,000 to my family life (trips, dinners, fun for kids, shopping for my wife). As I've grown, so have my goals, and yours should too.

For many of you, it will just start with, "What does it take to be free now?" The average median income is $45,000 per year. Let's say it is $48,000 which would break down to $4000 per month. For some of you, it can be much less. I have a friend who only needs enough to travel so he can surf, hike, and adventure. He lives out of a converted van and has found a way to generate around $2,500 a month and has a more fulfilling life then many CEOs making over six figures a year. $4,000 is really an easy number to generate. If you invest in real estate, that could be 20 units or one good commercial property. One small business with a system and process in place could create this kind of profit almost immediately. Or find a product to sell online for $20 that has a 20% return. You would only need to sell a thousand items a month. With a customer range of hundreds of millions online, how easy it is to sell a thousand items

.Find your freedom number and make it your absolute one thing. With the focus of a sniper, set your sight resolutely on it and in no time, you will reach the goal. What is also fun is as you start to build cashflow and your financial intelligence/creativity increase, you start to understand how easy it is to keep increasing your cashflow. Like me, once your goals increase or change, you'll see how easy it is for you to generate even more cashflow. Nothing will be out of your reach.

B. Understanding Good Debt – The Freedom from Bad Debt

This second concept is a tough one for many to swallow and understand. Debt tastes bitter and leaves our stomachs feeling queasy. And bad debt should. But there is a good debt. Bad debt is debt that doesn't produce anything and decreases your cashflow. For example, purchasing a TV on your credit card. Now you have a $1000 debt on your card at 12% interest. Each month that is a negative ding on your cashflow. It does nothing to help your one thing. Other things that are bad debt can be a car payment, school loans, financed trips, even a home loan can be considered bad debt since it doesn't produce.

Good debt is income producing debt. Many of you are like how is my home bad debt? I was told it's an asset? Well a home is not income producing, if you lost your job today can that home pay for itself? No! it cannot. But a good debt asset can. So I have some apartment complexes and they are all income producing, if I never went to work again they would continue to bring in income. Their income would pay the mortgage, taxes & insurance, maintenance, property management and profit into the bank account every month into forever.

Good debt is any debt that leads to profitable income production at the end of the month, vs bad debt which leads to negative production at the end of the month. The poor focus on paying off this bad debt. And it is a good thing not to have bad debt. But in focusing on paying off bad debt, they never increase their wealth through cashflow. The cards may be paid off, but when there is another emergency, they use up savings and then the cards are filled again, or a new loan is taken out. The wealthy instead build cash flowing assets through leverage of good debt and then use the new cashflow to hedge against things like emergencies, inflation, bills etc...

Don't worry so much about being debt free. Be bad debt-free, but learn how to creatively use good debt to your advantage. The wealthy do this and receive many benefits because of it. Too many to list here. As part of your growth and learning financial education, you will want to explore more books concerning this topic.

C. Know Your Worth – Freedom of Time

This one cannot be stressed enough. It also fits in with your one thing. As you build your focus on your one thing you will start to realize that things that don't fit into building your goals are no longer worth your time. You will no longer waste time trying to save pennies vs building systems that create dollars, or taking in gossip or drama.

As an example, I am an excellent painter – or at least I use to be before a car accident deprived me of a lot of the use in my right arm. Even with loss of use, I am still better than 90% of painters in my market. So because of this, even after I quit painting, I would still pick up jobs painting for years. Well recently my wife's best friend wanted her house painted. She begged me for months to do it. She finally negotiated that she will watch our kids for a weekend while the wife and myself go on a romantic getaway. Well even that still didn't make it worth my time. So I am paying a contractor friend almost $2,000 to paint here house. My time for two days is worth so much more than paying someone $2,000 to do a job for me.

Same goes in my businesses. I do not do the maintenance on my properties. Can I do plumbing work? Yes, I can, but it would take me a whole day to figure out a problem, when instead a plumber can fix it in 3 hours. If I fix the plumbing issue, I lose thousands of dollars in precious time. Where instead if I pay a plumber $300, I get my time, focus on other business, and I know it is being fixed right with a warranty.

You need to know your worth. So, you know when to start saying *no*.

At the beginning, yes, you will do more in your business to be successful. At some point though, you need to realize that hiring a professional will not only save time, but also money because they will do it quicker and do it right the first time (if you have a good contractor). So, while you have a professional doing a project for you, it frees you up to invest more in your business, yourself, or your family.

I was always the guy who helped friends move, fix something, paint, etc. It took a long time to realize my worth and start saying no to some of these things, but it's been so worth it to say no. Now I'm not saying become a complete jerked and never help your friends or family. So please understand the difference of when to help someone vs someone or something taking advantage of your time that could be used better elsewhere.

I have seen so many times in business where people try and save money by doing everything themselves. And because of this, it costs them more in the long run. To save $100, they will spend hours doing their bookkeeping and payroll, only to find mistakes at the end of the year. I've seen people stretch themselves so thin trying to do every position that they make huge mistakes like not delivering projects on time to customers, instead of hiring the right people for the right positions so the owner can focus on growing the business or other investments.

At the beginning of my real estate investing, I was the person to do everything. The maintenance was fine, but I made many expensive mistakes at management. I'd let rents slide, lose track of incoming money, and wouldn't properly vet tenants. These mistakes built up till I literally lost hundreds of thousands of dollars. Many of these mistakes were because I was stretched between my family, businesses, and properties.

Now if I would've understood my time's worth vs the cost of a property manager, I would've hired one at the very start. It would've saved so much money because they would've picked better tenants, collected rents on time, and handled maintenance faster. Plus, I would've had more time to invest into other businesses and real estate, increasing my cashflow and wealth.

CHAPTER 6
Make Your Money Work!

I know you bought this book to learn how to make money. Hopefully up to this point you have found value in the new concepts I have delivered to you. It is so important to understand what true wealth is, how to control your expenditures, and to have a proper mindset. Now you don't have to wait any longer. Let's start talking MONEY!

Our goal here is not to get you rich. It is to get you wealthy. We need to find ways for you to be able to grow a residual income that takes care of all your needs so you have your freedom. After that goal has been achieved, you will need to continue to grow your investments so your cashflow covers all your future wants as well. You cannot save your way to financial freedom. The reason we went over budgeting and saving was to find money, so we could start investing. The only way to financial freedom is through the compounding growth of your investments. This is how our money will do the work for us. It is how money becomes our slave even working while we sleep. How great would it be to go to bed every night and see your account has grown by morning?

Albert Einstein said **"Compound interest is the eighth wonder of the world. He who understands it, earns it…He who doesn't…pays it."**

Now I am sure we all can agree Mr. Einstein was a pretty smart man, so maybe we should take that to heart. What is compounding interest than? I will explain it simply. Simple interest is interest that does not get added to the principal (original amount), whereas compounding interest gets added to the principal sum of a loan or deposit. It becomes the result of adding to the principle by the interest being reinvested instead of paid out, in this way the interest in the next calculation period is earned on the principal sum plus the previously accumulated interest.

What does that mean in layman's terms? Let's look at an example. I have two sisters, so we will use two sisters for this. Rosa and Liz are both twenty-five. Rosa starts investing $3,600 annually and she does this until she is forty-five. Liz takes a little more time to wise up, she doesn't start until she is forty-five and she also invests $3,600 annually. Finally, at Seventy years old, Liz stops. They decide to compare their retirements. Each of them invested the same amount. Liz invested for five more years than Rosa did which is an extra $18,000 invested. Who do you think earned more?Rosa did. You see Rosa seized the "wonder" of compound interest. Her total was $1,307,903.16, whereas Liz, even though she invested more money with that extra five years, she only had $287,509.97. That is a $1,000,000 difference.

Rosa's money was able to keep working and growing without her continual investing. And with the power of compound interest, it was able to explode beyond what Liz's investment could even with more money invested. We see with this example the true power of compounding interest. We also see how important it is to start right now rather than later. So, let's look at the different ways to invest and have our money start working.

THE MARKET

The market can be both an exciting and scary place. In the market you can build wealth over time as in the example of the two sisters, make an incredible amount of money very fast, or lose it all overnight. Many investors stay away from the market because they have no control, or because it is not backed by a hard asset. The market, just like any other way to make money, is all part of the game. If you understand the rules of the game, you can win.

> "Rule No. 1: Never lose money. Rule No. 2: Never forget rule No. 1."
> – Warren Buffett

Now if only it was that easy, right? But it can be very simple again if you understand the rules and what to watch for. Most people make their first mistake by not trusting the correct "broker" financial advisor. I had a friend who was in a bad car accident about twelve years ago. She got almost ninety thousand dollars as a settlement. She tried to be smart with the money and took sixty thousand of it and had it invested. The problem was she didn't know what to look for in a "broker." She ended up going to the first office she found on google. Sadly, the gentleman she worked with had all kinds of fees and kept moving her money in and out of different investments, costing her everything.

Many brokerages are just like a casino. And as the saying goes, "the house never loses." They are setup to protect their own interests. They have all these different fees and programs to sell you on that make sure the company wins first. Well every percent compounded that is charged can erode your potential gains heavily over the years. In our example from before, if you added 1% more in a fee over the course of Rosa's investing, she would've made $901,690.39. That is $400,000 less with only 1% increase of fees. This is why it is very important to find the most reputable person to take care of your investing, if you are not able to do this on your own.

You want to find a financial advisor known as a "fiduciary." A fiduciary is required by law to put you first. A financial advisor that is a fiduciary made the decision to become one and they are known as an RIA (registered investment advisor). Because of their choice to become a fiduciary, they are required by law to put you first. If they sell you a stock in the morning at one price, but buy it that night at a better price, they have to give you their stock. When interviewing your fiduciary, you do need to make sure that they are independent and not a dually registered advisor.

The second step in market investing is having both understanding and patience with the market and its trends. Every year there is a correction in the market for the last one hundred years or so. A correction is a change in the market from 10-20%. There is also a bear market every five years or so. A bear market is a 20% or more correction. The problem with this is most people who invest and don't understand this get scared when it happens. Once the fear sets in, they sell off, losing everything or at least a bulk of it.

Now no one can truly predict the market, but we can see these trends. With seeing the trends of corrections and bear markets, we understand that as long as the economy grows, the market will rise at some point. After each bear market, a bull market has followed. So if you sell when the market falls and fear sets in, you will lose for sure. Those that fight the fear and stay in tend to win when the market goes back to bull.

Look at investors like Warren Buffet and Ronald Read. Neither one is known as an active trader. They are known as active buyers. For many of us it is hard to imagine ourselves in Warren Buffet's shoes, so let's look at Ronald Read. Ronald was a gas station attendant. Ronald was a man of very modest means. As you can imagine, a gas station clerk isn't the highest paid job out there. But that didn't stop him from acquiring an eight-million-dollar fortune. He was an active buyer who continued to buy and hold dividend stocks that allowed his investments to compound.

Through patience and time, no matter how much you currently make, you can turn it into a fortune. This leads to the third step in market investing: "building an investors mindset." I know we've already talked mindset stuff, but to be successful at anything the mind is where it always starts. If you are not mentally ready to be wealthy you will never obtain it, and if you are not mentally ready to invest and fight through the ups and downs, you will fail. Create a set of investment rules and follow them. Use it as a guide to keep you on track whenever things get tough, so you don't get emotional and make rash decisions with your investing.

Be open to seeking advice from opinions that differ from yours to make sure you are not falling into your own biases. I have seen people become so in love with a certain company that they have grown blind to warnings that it was time to move into something different. Patience and holding will win over short-term speculation, but sometimes there is a time to sell and invest elsewhere.

There is so much more to market investing than what we covered here. There are many great books to read on the matter as well as seasoned investors to follow and learn from, such as Warren Buffet, Carl Icahn, and Peter Mallouk. There are also great courses out there that can help teach you. As always, do your due diligence. I recommend a great friend of mine, Rizwan Memon, who runs Riz International, if you want to learn with the help of the pros.

REAL ESTATE INVESTING

Now if you want to build some wealth with confidence and speed, this is a great place to do it. I will never call anything easy, but I will say real estate is a simple and proven method to acquire wealth. I personally know more financially free millionaires from real estate than I do from any other industry. I personally have invested in residential, multifamily, apartments, commercial, and land holdings.

Some of the bonuses of real estate are:

- It is a hard physical asset. Unlike stocks, real estate, like an apartment, is tangible. As long as it doesn't burn down or fly away in a tornado, your investment is always there. People always need a roof over their head.

- People don't always need to buy a home, but people almost always need to rent a home. When 2008 happened, the investors that lost the most in real estate were the flippers and real estate agents. The people who continued to do great were the buy-and-hold investors.

Just like we discussed about the stock market, holding on for the long term in real estate can almost always create a win. The flippers couldn't sell during the crash and usually had investors or the bank they needed to pay back right away. The buy-and-hold investor, however, just continued to rent like they always did. Sure in some markets they may have had to lower rents to where they only broke even, but over time the market came back and rents went up. Now those buy-and-hold investors have a cashflow-positive property and more equity in the property.

- It has multiple ways to increase in value or hedge against inflation. With a rental property, every time a tenant makes a payment, it pays down the principle amount, which increases your equity over time. It is like a long-term savings account that someone else is depositing into for you.

Overtime the property will also go up in value, which is more money being thrown into your savings account. The increased value also brings in increased rents. All of this becomes a hedge against inflation. With a savings, every year your money sits there, inflation steals from it. But real estate fights against inflation by growing income, value, and savings.

It is also residual. Which is our main goal with investing. We want our time and freedom. Properly managed real estate can provide you that freedom with monthly mailbox money so you can focus on what is truly important in your life.

- It has multiple exit strategies. If you own a retail business, your strategy is to take product or service and sell it. If it doesn't sell, then you are pretty limited on what you can do. With real estate though, you have so many strategies. Here are a few. You can rent the property and make an income. The property can be sold retail for a profit. If you need to, you can owner-finance it to someone. You can do a lease option. Real estate comes with so many strategical options to help protect your investment.

You can invest in it with no money, or at least none of your own. I love this part of real estate and this will be our focus of this section. Unlike other things like investing in the market, going to college, or creating a product, you can literally get into real estate investing with none of your own money. This is not one of those Saturday night infomercials. This is legit real estate fact!I have closed on single family homes all the way up to multi-million-dollar commercial properties with none of my own money. The secret to this is finding people with a problem and then creatively bringing them a solution. It is really that simple.Imagine you have a neighbor named Frank who owns a fourplex. He bought it for cashflow to help his retirement. He is older though and has not been able to keep up on the maintenance and is also having trouble getting tenants to pay on time. He wants the monthly income but cannot deal with the stress anymore.

So, you go over and chat with Frank, learning all these issues. Well because of your financial creativity and education, you have some solutions. You make a couple offers and one he is really interested in. He will owner-finance the place to you for an agreed amount on a thirty-year note. In return, you will take over all the maintenance and tenant issues, and you will pay him each month on time just as you would the bank. Now Frank can enjoy his retirement years without the stress of managing a property and yet still collect some monthly income.

I have used this same strategy many times. This works for SFH, multifamily, even the commercial space. We found an office building/strip mall that had tired owners. Because of bad maintenance practices, they were never able to leave town to see their grandkids for fear something would happen to the property. They also were worried about selling the property because they had owned it so long and depreciated it. They were going to have to pay a hefty tax bill.So, we figured out their pain points and how much money they needed a month to start enjoying life. With that information, we negotiated a deal where they owner financed the property on a thirty-year note. Now I have a great cash-flowing asset and they have the freedom to leave town without worrying.

This is a very small part of real estate investing strategies. I recommend reading books such as the *Rich Dad Poor Dad* series, as well as listening to podcasts such as *Bigger Pockets* and *The Cashflow Guys Podcast*. It's also a good idea to find a mentor who has been doing true real estate investing (not a mls buyer) with financial creativity to learn from. Start going to local investor meetups through your local REIA group, or find some on meetup.com or Facebook. If you cannot find someone local to learn from, I also recommend checking out *The Kingdom Real Estate*, *Cashflow Guys Mailbox Mastermind*, or ChrisRood.com. I have personally worked with each of these guys in some capacity and out of the sea of fake gurus out there, these three companies are the real deal and will help you on your journey.

BUSINESS INVESTING

For millions of people, starting your own business has been the American dream. To be in control of one's own income and time is the pinnacle of success. The great thing is we live in a time and age where there is so much opportunity to start a business. And not just a local mom-and-pop, but an international force of capitalism.

Business is my most favorite form of investing. Like real estate, it also has different options on how to get involved. Some of these options you can do with no money as well. Owning a business also comes with a lot of prestige. As someone who owns millions of dollars of real estate, I can tell you very few people are ever impressed when we talk about it, but when we discuss business, you can always see people light up and get excited.

So, like the other types of investments we discussed, I am going to just highlight a few different styles of businesses and how to get involved in them. There are so many different types of businesses and strategies to go with them it would almost take a series of books to cover it all.

Ecommerce

Ecommerce is the new brick-and-mortar. Ecommerce has a few huge benefits over the traditional brick-and-mortar though. With a typical B&M, you are limited to being open a certain amount of hours, a certain amount of days, and to a limited amount of people in your region. With ecommerce you now have a store selling twenty-four hours a day around the world to hundreds of millions of clients.

You can see over the last couple years strong brands we grew up with like Toys R Us, K Mart, Hastings, and Blockbuster have all gone out of business. B&M has setup costs of location, high rents, utilities, NNN fees…it all adds up. Ecommerce has a low cost in comparison. You can run it from a laptop in your bed. And with drop shipping, you don't even have to purchase inventory to start.

Drop shipping, if you haven't heard of it, is a method of ecommerce that involves selling product on your store that gets fulfilled from a third-party supplier directly to the consumer. This is a great way to get started if you have little to no money.

Drop shipping gives you almost an endless selection of products. You won't have to worry about logistics, tracking inventory, managing stock levels. It is a great way to start and learn what works and sells. Drop shipping does come with some disadvantages. Drop shipping has low margins. There can be supplier errors and inventory issues all out of your control. It also is not a long-term, sustainable business model, but it is a great way to help build your brand. What I recommend is learning how to dropship via YouTube videos and free ecommerce groups on Facebook. Then pick a product niche that you have some understanding of. From there, go on Shopify and start your account. They even give a free two-week trial.

As your sales grow, you will start to see what items are good, and which are not. Take the top sellers and get them branded from the manufacturer with a logo of your design. Start another store and start putting your own branded material on there. As you build that up, you will have a strong, great-margined, long-term business. This is a great strategy to start yourself a company with little investment and little risk.

Traditional Business

There are so many different options between sales, service, retail, food, and manufacturing that it can be hard to decide. Most likely, if you want to start a business you already have an idea of what you understand and can build a business around. It helps on the road.

1. An Idea

All businesses start with an idea. If you already have one, great. If not, it can be hard to come up with one. I usually recommend people start looking at things they enjoy. If we can find something you already love to do and turn it into a business, the chance of you succeeding at it increases. It's more likely you will push harder and fight through the lean times doing something you love over just running a business you started because it was recommended to you.

When deciding on an idea, look for solutions to a problem as well. Is there something in your market people are always saying they wish they had? Are there companies that are lacking in a service that you can provide? Maybe you can do something other people are already doing, but you can do it faster.

2. Create a Plan

A business plan can be so helpful in both starting your business and keeping it on track. For my first business, we did not have a plan, and it showed. For my second business, we did have a plan, and both had incredible growth. Your plan should help you define some key questions such as, "Who is our market?" "What is our offering?" and "What are our long term goals?" Finding the answer to these questions will help the start of your company's trajectory and long-term direction. In your plan, you will also want to define your management setup – who is in charge of what. Plan out your twelve-month budget and pro forma. And figure out your funding for the project.

There are many great sites to find sample business plans on, or you can look locally by contacting your local SBA. At the SBA, you will find older gentleman that have run businesses for years and are donating their time to help others formulate a business plan. Most of these gentleman are only minorly successful on the self-employed scale, so don't take everything they say to heart. You want to learn from the top people in your field, not some local guy who ran his mom-and-pop and never grew beyond it. But these guys will be good to help you with a business plan.

3. Financing

While building your plan, you should have obtained a great understanding of what you need to finance this endeavor. Depending on what type of business it is, it could cost anywhere from hundreds of dollars to hundreds of thousands.

But don't let something like cost deter you. I sold my car to fund my first business, and after about eight months of proving ourselves, my grandma and my business partner's mom each gave us an extra ten thousand to scale. I had no money to start my second business. We had lost everything due to some law changes and bad partnership. A friend who saw what I did with the first business gave us ten thousand dollars for ten percent equity. My partner and myself bootstrapped that business living on the floor of the backroom, and over three years, turned it into a million-dollar business spread over multiple states. Both of those businesses should have been started with a hundred grand easily. I came from homelessness, so I obviously didn't have the money to get them going. But with sacrifice and hard work, we made it happen.

Even if you don't have a car to sell or a friend to borrow from, you can still make it happen. When we went through your finances you should have found anywhere from an extra two hundred to eight hundred dollars a month to free up. Start each month taking some of that money either save it or invest it in some retail arbitrage or selling free craigslist items. In a few months you will have enough to start something and change your destiny.

You can also put some of that financial creativity we talked about in real estate towards a business. Find a business that is for sale and meet with the owner. Find out why he is selling and see if there are some problems you can help solve. Maybe he loves the business but is getting to old but would still enjoy a steady check. Many small business owners are just like the real estate owners. They have a problem and if you can help them solve it, you can create opportunity for yourself.

4. Get the Word Out

Once you start a business, go get your name out there. Most traditional business owners, or worse, the "local marketers," will tell you to advertise on TV, radio, or local papers, etc. Stay away from all that. Once you open your doors, every marketer in town will be knocking on your door begging for your money while offering nothing in return but empty promises (I'm probably not making any friends with radio advertisers here).

There are much better and more cost-effective ways to get the word out. Social media is one of the first things I recommend. It is so cheap or even free. You can do ads for pennies of what TV or radio would cost. You also can track how effective it is whereas you really cannot with traditional advertising. You also are able to leverage your audience. Start adding friends in your market or your targeted clientele. From there, make sure to be posting and talking about your business. Let everyone know who you are and what you do.

Door to door is my next recommendation. Now I don't mean door knocking unless your target business is stay-at-home clients. What I mean is going directly to local businesses that may be your target clientele. When I had my marijuana stores, we would go directly to doctor's offices and explain what we do and how we can help their patients. We would get client referrals from then on. With our cellular repair stores, we would visit all local businesses that we knew relied on a phone like realtors, accountants, medical personnel, and security.

There is a restaurant chain called *Texas Road House*, and they have mastered these strategies. They don't advertise. Instead they take their delicious rolls with butter and go daily handing them out at different businesses. In my town, they are the biggest restaurant because of this.

5. BUSINESS SETUP

I am not a CPA or a lawyer, nor will I pretend either. I strongly recommend that you do not setup your company on your own. Go sit down with a professional and discuss the benefits and negatives between the corporate structures. I will say stay away from a sole proprietorship, and you should just walk away from any expert who recommends it. For your tax professional, you do not want someone who is just resting on what they learned in college.

Choose someone who is actively studying and finding ways to help their clients with tax strategies.Also, hire a bookkeeper or have your accountants in house take care of it. Your time is worth so much more to your business than trying to figure out the books. I've seen so many people, myself included, lose money because of trying to do everything themselves.I recommend reading *Tax-Free Wealth* by Tom Wheelright, or taking a course by Mark Kohler. I can also recommend both of Mark Kohler's companies "kkoslawyers.com" and "kohlereyercpas.com" for consulting on your setups if you cannot find good local representation.

6. Develop a Team

So many small business owners fail because of this. They have this notion that no one is trustable, or if you want something done right, you do it yourself. Because of that mindset they are never able to grow or scale, and never able to have time for a vacation or time with friends or family.

Look at Ray Kroc. Do you think he ever worried about hiring a manager and whether or not they would collapse his business? No! He hired and fired as needed, always putting the right people in positions he knew weren't his best fit. McDonalds would not be where it is today if it wasn't for team building. That goes for every other major company out there. If you want to just be a successful mom-and-pop that employs your kids to do all the crap work and never have anytime, then don't build a team. But if you want to grow and have both money and time, you will have to build a team. Placing the correct people in the right positions will save both time and money.

I was in charge of bookkeeping at my cellular stores. When my dad passed away, I quit paying attention to the books for a while, which gave one of our managers the opportunity to steal more than thirty thousand dollars. If I would've had a bookkeeper in place, this incident would have been caught sooner. I also would have been able to spend more time growing my company instead of trying to be a bookkeeper.

As with the other things we have talked about, there is so much to opening and running a business. These are some starter points that I hope will really help you on your journey. Some books I recommend are, *32 Ways to Be a Champion in Business* by Magic Johnson, *The Power of Broke* by Daymond John, and *Third Circle Theory* by Pejman Ghadimi. Also check out *The MFCEO Podcast* with Andy Frisella (warning: language) and *The Profit* TV show. It is like getting mentored by some of the greatest business minds out there for free.

CHAPTER 7
Focus Your Effort

I work with a lot of entrepreneurs and investors. While doing this, I have been able to see a constant in the habits of those that are successful and the ones that are not. It's the ability to focus and master one thing. We all have heard the statistic that millionaires have an average of seven streams of income. Because of this, many of the people I work with have all immediately jumped into multiple investments. Since they haven't fully mastered their first thing yet, taking on the extra investments usually leads to stress and unwise financial choices. It will spread them too thin.

You look at a guy like Richard Branson who has ownership in more than four hundred companies. Richard did not immediately open all these companies. He started in 1972 with one company, growing and scaling it until the time was right for a second company. Richard also didn't just open up whatever the next hot idea was. Instead he opened up a company that worked with his current business, adding another leg of revenue.

When a newer entrepreneur immediately goes after new revenue streams, it can lead to many problems.

1. The business is not ready for them to focus in other areas. You only have so much time and cannot do everything. Without proper systems in place, a company without its owner's full attention will start to waiver.

2. Markets go up and down all the time. If you have spread your money out too early and the market goes slow, how will your business be able to get through it? It is so important to have proper funds and reserves before spreading to multiple investments.
3. Everything is so competitive and changing at light speeds. We are at an age where everything is becoming so specialized. It can be almost impossible to compete in varying fields. Without enough knowledge of your new investment, or the ability to hire someone for it, you will fail.

The rich man I worked for, the one I talked about in early chapters, didn't understand any of this. He did not believe in systems or hiring experts to run positions in his company. He would continuously open new businesses without any knowledge of the field except knowing other people make money in it. After a while, he just didn't have enough time to run everything and it all fell apart around him. I was able to learn from his examples on what not to do. Instead, I focused on my business, insuring it had a strong foundation, a team that worked together, and a management structure to lead it. We spent year one reinvesting everything back into the business to make sure it had a strong base. Our second year we grew the company to multiple stores to widen its foundation.

In year three, I was able to start investing into new revenue streams without fear of my main income being compromised. I started investing in real estate so I could grow my residual income. Real estate comes with its own problems and learning curves. At this point in time, I did not have a mentor to ask advice of, so I made mistakes in the beginning. If my main business would not have been so strong, I would have lost everything. But because I had mastered my first stream of income, it was able to carry me through learning and building my second stream.

You ever notice when people try and get fit, and after a couple weeks it gets hard and they quit? There are a few reasons this happens, but focus is a big part. You see, people will change their diet to an extreme they are not use to. They will start working out much harder than they are ready for. They will also begin waking up at much earlier hours, usually to fit the workout in. With all of these extremes introduced at one time, their body breaks down. They feel tired, sore, and usually sick from diet change. So, the first thing they do is go back to their old ways of lounging around, eating hot wings, and watching Netflix marathons.

Now if they just focused on one thing at a time, how much better the success rate would be. Instead of extreme diet and workout change, imagine just changing the diet while adding in walking or a mild jog daily. It would give them the time to fight through diet sickness without also dealing with muscle soreness. Once the diet is in check, then add the full physical workouts. The success rate rises dramatically in those who focus on one thing first over those that take on too much right out of the gate. I want you to be free. I want you to have multiple streams of income flowing into your lake of wealth. But it is important that you do it the right way.

Remember, slow and steady wins the race. Warren Buffet didn't make his wealth overnight. It was done through consistent and responsible trading over many years. He focused on becoming a master in one area. It was not until much later that he started to buy other companies to hold as investments. Be like Warren Buffet or Richard Branson and focus on your one thing first. Grow it while putting systems in place, and once it is strong, then look for other investments.

CHAPTER 8
PROTECT YOUR WEALTH

I was having a really hard time writing this chapter. It is not easy to write about all the boring stuff like insurance. We had a scare tonight though that really put into perspective how important this chapter is. I was sitting in my living room while the kids were eating dinner. I have four boys: Jax, nine: Abel, eight; Gabriel, six; and Ryker, five. Well, Gabriel comes running to find me. His face is turning purple from choking. Immediately I begin to give him the Heimlich maneuver. We are able to get his throat cleared by the grace of God. I am not going to lie though, I was scared. I remained calm, but my heart rate and emotions were high. He teared up and hugged me as I held him so tight that we were lucky I didn't suffocate him.

This moment showed that at any time, we could lose someone we love or something we have worked so hard for. Protecting our wealth, businesses, and loved ones is so important because we are not always in control. My first business was in the marijuana industry, and we had entire crops fail, robberies, and inside theft. Man plans, and God laughs, which means we are not in control. So why not protect ourselves? I have insurance on all of my children, my wife, and myself.

I told an investor friend of mine I had life insurance on each of my kids, and he responded with, "I don't think I would feel good making money off the death of one of my children." Now I don't have this hoping I get rich off of losing one of them, but instead I have it so we can be with each other through the loss and mourning without worrying about going back to work. I can take the time to make sure my family is healed before returning to the normal daily grind. How much better would it be to have finances taken care of while you tend to your loved one's pain, instead of having to hurry back to work?

The four most common types of insurance are health insurance, property and business liability insurance, auto insurance, and life insurance.

1. Health Insurance

Your health should be your number one priority. As we discussed earlier in this book, what is the point of building wealth and freedom if you are so weak and sick you cannot enjoy it? Having a good diet and workout regimen are super important, but things outside our control even happen to our bodies. And when something happens, many people, even the wealthy, are scared to go to the doctor's office for fear of the cost and the result. Well insurance can't help with fear of the doctor, but it can help with the cost of the visit. According to AARP, the average cost of treatment for cancer is $150,000. That's a lot of cash that would be better put to use growing in more investments instead of padding a drug company's budget.

2. Property and Business Insurance

In 2013, a seventy-one-year old lady went grocery shopping. Another customer was using a motorized shopping cart and ended up running into the elderly lady, pushing her head-first and four feet deep into a shelving unit. Instead of suing the operator, she sued the store. She won her case on the grounds that the store didn't do its duty to make sure customers who operated the carts had enough training to do so. That is ludicrous on so many levels, but it is the state of the society we are in. I recommend always having your properties and business insured because you just never know what could happen. A tenant could spill water on their floor and a guest could fall on it. Who are they going to go after – their friend, or the huge landowner who has all the money in the world? What if you have a product-based business and a leak in the roof happens, ruining a majority of your product? Protect yourself and your assets.

3. Auto Insurance

This one I will not spend much time on. It's a law everywhere as far as I know. Plus, vehicular accidents happen all the time. In 2012, I was in two car accidents thirty days apart. One morning I was headed to help a friend when a big red truck ran a red light and t-boned my little Honda Civic. Thirty days later, I was in my wife's car waiting in a turn lane when a drunk driver hit me head on. I lost about 30% of the movement in my right arm and a majority of the feeling and grip in it. Thank God they were both insured and were able to take care of my medical bills and rehabilitation, especially since that was after I lost my first business. If, for some reason, they would not have had any insurance, it still would have worked out because I was insured.

4. Life Insurance

Most people look at life insurance as a big scam. How can someone insure something like death when we know it is inevitable? It makes the average person wonder, "How does an insurance company make money insuring a guaranteed claim?"

I'm not going to go into all of that. Instead we will discuss how to leverage life insurance to help control and build your wealth.

You have two main types of life insurance: *term* and *whole life* or *permanent* insurance. Term insurance is the typical way people get life insurance. It has a set term for how long the product is good for whether it is ten years, twenty, or even thirty years. If the purchaser dies while in effect, then the beneficiary will receive the sum of term insurance that was purchased. This is great for providing protection in case of death for your loved ones to be able to pay off debt and have money for funeral. Most people, however, outlive their term policy and to get another. It is usually more expensive due to the increased age or worsened health of the individual. The term policy is cheaper than the whole life policy, but it has limitations and doesn't come with some of the benefits to leverage.

Whole life or permanent is the one I want to really discuss. Whole life has great benefits in that everything is fixed and guaranteed. Your death benefits, the monthly cost – all guaranteed in the contract. Even the cash value is guaranteed.

What is the "cash value?" As you pay your monthly premium, a portion is paid into an investment account. Overtime, this grows with both interest and your monthly payments. This is money you can claim by cashing out and surrendering your policy early, subtracting whatever fees. However, with the living benefits of the policy, you have access to low percentage or even zero-interest tax-free loans. It is these loans that give us the great leverage I mentioned.

You may have heard of infinite banking before. Here is an explanation, if not a very simplistic one: **Using the tax-free loan from the earnings growth that has been built into your life insurance policy to invest in** a higher percentage return asset allows you to pay yourself back with interest. In this way you are increasing your net-worth with new a asset, increasing your income from the asset, and increasing your policy savings with interest collected. A bank lends you money and charges interest, making back what they loaned by almost double in some cases. With this strategy, you are now the bank.

Example: You find a property to flip for $80,000 and it takes $20,000 to remodel. So, you get a loan from the bank for $100,000 at 6% interest on a twenty-year term. It takes you one year to sell the house for $120,000. At this point, you will have paid back the bank the $100,000 plus a total of $5,927.37 in interest.

Now through the whole life policy you will get a much better interest rate at 2-4%, and some policies will even do 0% after a certain amount of years holding the policy. So, let's look at the same project with this strategy at 3%. You borrow the $100,000 at 3% interest instead of the 6%. It takes you still one year to sell, but this time instead of paying back a total of $105,927.37 to a bank, you pay back to your policy $102,702.38. That's $3,224.99 in extra profit. Most of the investors I know take that extra earning and pay it into their policy as if they charged themselves 6% in interest. But you see how borrowing from yourself this way can help build your wealth at a faster rate than working with banks. It also puts you in a position where you don't have to wait for bank approval.

There is one more added benefit which adds to the infinite banking part of this strategy. If your agent has set you up properly, you will have the ability to get what is called a "participating loan." With the first example, when you borrow the money out of the policy it doesn't keep collecting interest, but with the spread loan it continues to earn interest from the insurance company continuing to invest with it also. So let's say you borrow that same money at 5% on a spread loan. The insurance company continues to invest it, making back the average return S&P 10 year of 7.67%. That is a 2.67% increase. Now add that to the 10-20% return you get from the property you flipped and you will see how simple it is for you to grow your wealth infinitely.

There is way more to insurance strategies than what we have discussed here. I recommend asking your agent questions involving these strategies and seeing what they say. There are also some great reading materials in books like *Become Your Own Bank, the Infinite Banking Concept* by R. Nelson Nash, or anything by Mark Kohler, who also has some great educational videos on the matter. You can find those on YouTube or his website. Another great resource is a friend of mine, Mike Gillum, at createtailwind.com. Beyond insurance, you also want to be very mindful of your structuring of businesses and holding companies. It is so important to have the right kind of business structure to help protect you from lawsuits and set you up for better tax rates. I am not a CPA or a business lawyer, so I will not go too heavily into all of this. I do recommend that you do your research before deciding on a lawyer and CPA to bring onto your team. The majority of CPAs only do what they were taught in college and have not actually researched what it takes to benefit their clients and help them out with strategies that the wealthy use. I have seen so many people with million-dollar companies that are setup as a sole-proprietorship just waiting to get into a law suit and lose it all.

If the lawyer or accountant you work with even mentions that setup, just walk out. You want to work with someone who can explain the benefits of an L.L.C., S-corp, C-corp, and why you would want an

L.L.C. taxed as a S-corp or C-corp. The professional will discuss with you a L.L.C known as Charging Owner Protection Entity or COPE entity. The professional you talk to should be discussing strategies such as land trusts, living will, and SDIRAs.

There are so many things to add to your structure to protect your family and the generational wealth you have built for them. It is so important to learn all you can in these areas to ensure that the professionals you hire are doing the right things and making sure you are protected. Again, a majority of the professionals don't understand this stuff. They are just self-employed, broke-minded professionals. You need someone who understands these concepts because they are also building their own wealth and using these strategies.

CHAPTER 9
PLAN YOUR DREAMS AND SEIZE THEM

For many Americans, the dream is to become debt-free, have $500,000 to a million dollars in the account, and be retired by 65, taking it easy. If this is still you, I want you to go into your shower, turn the water onto cold, and bang your head against the wall till you pass out or you have a mindset shift. I get so angry thinking about people wasting their lives at forty to sixty hours a week for forty to fifty years just to have a couple years of rest before death.

God didn't spend six days creating all the wonders of this Earth for us not to explore them. He didn't give us the brains and imaginations we have to waste them away in a cubicle and then go on autopilot till death. Why settle for so little when you can have so much more? You can have it all. And more importantly, you can help improve the rest of the world if you use everything we have talked about in this book and build a real plan and legacy.

Grant Cardone released a video in which he said, "If you have a million dollars saved up for retirement, you're a deadbeat." And you know what? He was right. A million dollars in the next twenty to forty years is nothing. Every day the powers that be continue to steal from you through inflation and mismanagement of the U.S. economy. What is worse is many people won't even have a million dollars for retirement. They will be living off of whatever socialistic program that has been setup for them. Who wants such a meager life in their final years? Hopefully not you. This is why you must do what the wealthy do. You have to plan your dream retirement, your dream life, your empire now, and start making the sacrifices to get there.

I have shown you in this book the steps to take to make the income for anything you want in life. Whatever you want in your future, you can have. Now that you have had some financial education and your eyes have been opened to the matrix, you should see nothing but possibilities. You can even turn things that would normally be a liability into an asset. Imagine you want to spend half the year in the north and the other half the year down south. Well by a place in each location that you could turn into an Airbnb and rent out when you're not using it. Now that house that would normally be a liability, that you're making payments on, is now paying for itself as well as building equity and possibly even some cashflow.

A mentor of mine, Pejman Ghadimi, has two courses called *Exotic Car Hacks* and *Watch Conspiracy* where he teaches how to properly buy an exotic car or high-end watch, be able to use it, and then sell it for a profit later. So, again with taking in financial education and having a proper mindset, you can have all you want and make money off of it, too. I have another friend who owns a private jet and has a renting system for it, so it pays for itself. The possibilities are endless. Now I want you to plan your dreams. With having your mind open, you should have more of an idea of what you truly want and how to get there. I want you to start a dream board.

On the dream board, put all your wants. Put the house you want, the vacation property, the car, helicopter, whatever it is, put it on there. After all that I want you to also add a mission or charity that you believe in and would love to support. It is very important that you have something more to live for than just yourself. It's great to have all these wants and to fulfill them, but it is even greater and more fulfilling to give and bless others. I also recommend taking a picture of it and making it your background on your phone or screen saver so it is always there at the front of your mind. I do this with my dream board and my weekly to do list. With the dream board made, I next want you to make a plan on how to achieve these dreams. This can be put on a board or even written out – whatever works for you. I have mine on a marker board in my office. So many people fail when making a plan because they don't break it down. They put down massive goals and a timeline to when they want it, but they don't make a realistic step-by-step on how to get there.

For the plan I like to start with the end, which is, let's say, your dream board. So, we know that you are headed to X, now how many years to get there? Figure out what works for you. I personally did a ten-year plan because I was ready to be done. With knowing your end date, start working backwards: "To be here in ten, I need this to be my five-year goal," "To hit this in five years, I need to be here in two years." From the two year point, you need to start breaking it down into way more detail. So, you will write out what are you going to do this week and each week for month one, and then the goals for month two. Then write out what you need to hit by month six and then your one year.

It is so important to write out and plan your goals in a realistic fashion. Each goal should be a step towards reaching an ultimate goal. So if your goal is, "I want to have $40,000 profit in residual income a month by owning two hundred units," you cannot make that your only goal. I see people all the time put up this one huge goal, and when they don't achieve it in the first couple months, they quit. Instead, if your goal is two hundred units, put it like this "I will start a course and/or hire a mentor and go through it all weeks one through two. Week three I will start marketing and door knocking. Week four I will build a team. Month two I will close my first property. Month three I will close my first multi-family. By six months, I will have 40 units. At 1 year, we will have built up to 80 units and by the end of year two, I will have 200 units."

Obviously, you will add more detail into each week by saying what exactly you are doing each day that week. But this should give you an idea of how to see your goal and start breaking it down to actionable and realistic steps to achieve your goals.

As you are building your dream board and setting these goals, make sure to involve those around you. If you are married, it is so important to be on the same page and build the dream together, which will strengthen your relationship. If you have kids, have them help you and work with you. Children crave their parent's attention, and if you lead and teach them, they will grow up to be duplicates of you, so use an opportunity like this to put them on a great path.

I hope this book has opened your eyes to what wealth truly is and how to start moving to obtain it. It doesn't matter how much you currently make. We have shown you it is possible for you to break out of the rat race and achieve everything you could ever want. You can do everything the wealthy can do. You can own your time and be free.

Notes

Notes

Notes

Notes

Notes

Notes

Notes

Notes

Notes

Made in the USA
Columbia, SC
05 May 2019